10 REASONS WHY YOU ARE YET TO START A BUSINESS

Identifying the blocks stopping you from taking a step

FRANCIS ELIAS

Copyright © 2024 Francis Elias

Self-published on Amazon KDP

All rights reserved. No part of this book may be reproduced, distributed, or transmitted in any form or by any means, including photocopying, recording, or other electronic, digital or mechanical methods, without the prior written permission of the publisher/author, except in the case of brief quotations embodied in critical reviews and certain other, write to the publisher/author via the email; eliasfrancis735@gmail.com

DEDICATION

I dedicate this book to my son, Joshua Francis.

CONTENTS

Dedication

Content

Introduction

Reason 1

Reason 2

Reason 3

Reason 4

Reason 5

Reason 6

Reason 7

Reason 8

Reason 9

Reason 10

Summary

5

INTRODUCTION

You are welcome!

First, I don't want you to read this book. Yes. I want us to have a discussion instead. Reading is sometimes boring. A discussion seems better. But if reading is better for you, it's okay by me too.

Second, if you know that after having this discussion, you will not apply whatever you discover to your business, project, career, etc. let's not have the discussion. There is no point learning what you will not use to attract a change.

Third, I am not perfect. So, if in case you see any spelling error, kindly grab the message, and move on. I've gone through this discussion countless times and had other people do same, plus, the editor. However, we are all humans, and there may still be a few errors.

Lastly, I want to congratulate you for being here. It shows that you are already a success, so, I await the testimonies soonest.

Having said that, let's jump into the topic; **"Ten Reasons Why You Are Yet To Start A Business"**

REASON 1

YOU HAVE NOT DECIDED TO START A BUSINESS

Have you heard of the popular saying that decision makes men?

It's okay to desire becoming a business owner, but, until you decide you won't be able to start.

In my place of work, some of my colleagues talked about saving money from their salaries so they can start small businesses, but year-in year-out, none have resigned yet. This was 2022 and it's 2024 already (as at when this book was written) but nothing yet. Whenever they talk about business, I would give them tips on how they should go about it. Some would even write the tips down - but no action.

Wanting to start a business is one step, **deciding to start** is another step. *Where are you right now?* It is not enough to wish; you must make it a decision.

See my experience;

My friend, Prince Ahiauzu and I talked about starting a consultancy business *(partnership)* since 2020, but we didn't do anything about it until 2022 after my NYSC. We met and started looking for shop to rent. Guess what? We didn't have even one naira at this time.

What changed? A **decision** came in. To surprise you, we didn't get the shop, rather, we made our homes the offices. That's all.

That's the power of decision. Once you decide it in your mind, everything about you will swing to action. *Just* **DECIDE** *first.*

REASON 2

YOU DON'T KNOW WHY YOU WANT TO START A BUSINESS

A friend told me she wants to start a business. I asked her why? And she said she wants to be her own boss. I smiled and told her to go back and think again. She never came back with that discussion again, maybe she never really had a good reason.

This is another aspect most small business owners gets it wrong. The three common reasons why people start small businesses are; for passion, to be a self-boss, and to make money (become a millionaire).

This is not to validate any of the reasons above whether good or not, no. This is for you to understand your driving force. But, if you must choose, I recommend passion and making money together. Be in business to make as much money as possible, through any means legal.

Ask yourself questions like; Why do I want to start a business? Which niche can I do better? etc.

See an illustration:

Q: Why do I want to start a business?

Ans: To make as much money as possible (to become a millionaire)

Q: Which niche can I do better?

Ans: Business consulting and information selling

Q: Where can I succeed in this business?

Ans: Online and my physical environment.

Until you are clear about why you want to start a business, you may not really start it until you are old. Then, it'll be a story about a dream that never came through.

REASON 3

YOU HAVE A JOB YOU ARE DOING NOW!

As much as it is good to have a job and still be successful (make money), it is another reason you are yet to take a step.

I know many people say that employed jobs cannot make you rich, however, it depends. There are a few jobs out there that can make you a millionaire. Despite this, your current employment is still a reason you are yet to start a business.

I watched a Nollywood movie – I can't recall the title but it's about a *one-night stand* - where a young man explained that he just woke up one morning and resigned from his good paying job just to start a tech company.

He always wanted to own a business but never made the decision when to do so. The day he decided, he quit his job immediately and went on to establish the business.

You see that decision came in first, followed by job quitting.

Now, I'm not saying you should quit your job immediately, No. What I am saying here is that; you should decide when you want to start and work on it. Sometimes you don't even need to quit your job yet, depending on the type of business you have in mind.

So, I believe you are clear now, right?

REASON 4

YOU ARE AFRAID OF LOSSING!

Honestly, this is one risk almost every intending business owner is afraid of – the possibility of experiencing loss.

I wish I can guarantee you a loss free business or investment experience, but I can't. Though, I've never experienced loss in my business life. I've worked in several companies, both big and small, but the least profit I've ever reported was 15% and it was once as a fast-food branch manager. Others were 20%+ profits. Despite this experience, I still can't give you a 100% loss free business.

Yes, your reason is to make money, but not to experience loss is also not a reason you should start a business.

Some businesses are highly profitable, while some are not so profitable. It depends on the type of business you are looking to start.

A colleague once confessed that it's not easy to start a business. She explained that the stress of going to market to buy materials, cook food, and sell was too risky. What if nobody comes to buy? It means that she would end up having a huge loss. That was her fear.

Just like my colleague, you are also afraid of loss that's why you are still here. Fear is **False Evidence Appearing Real**. You've allowed false evidence to appear and become real in your life.

Sometimes this fear comes from self-doubt and low self-esteem. You feel like you can't do it, and as a result, it's now a reality that you never took a step.

What should you do? Remove fear. It is okay to fail and try again.

REASON 5

LACK OF INFORMATION ABOUT YOUR CHOICE BUSINESS

Of course, you can't start a business you don't have a good knowledge about. It will be unwise except if you are to partner with someone you trust that knows better about such business idea. If not, then this is one of the reasons you have not been able to start a business.

However, not having enough knowledge about a particular business comes from somewhere. This may include:

1. Not reading business books and contents.
2. Not attending business events e.g. seminars, workshops, etc.

3. Not surrounding yourself with business-oriented persons.
4. Not attending webinars (online business meetings)

All these are habits that limits your business knowledge. But, if you turn them around, they are recommended processes you can gain business knowledge and skills to start and manage any business. In addition, there are a lot of online tools and platforms you can use to gain such knowledge. This may include:

- YouTube
- Google
- AI, such as Chat GPT
- LinkedIn

All these are available and free for your use. You only need an internet enabled device, that's all.

REASON 6

YOU ARE WAITING FOR GOVERNMENT GRANTS AND SUPPORTS FROM FAMILY

This more common among other reasons.

You hear people giving excuses that the government has not created an enabling environment for small business to thrive. That government are not helping, and even when they do, they still give it to their relatives. My uncle is rich, but he doesn't want to help. And so on...

Yes, as a Nigerian, we all know it is not easy. But will you also wait for the government to come sweep your room and arrange the bed you slept last night on? If not, then you are to a greater extent responsible for anything that happens to you.

I know there are some situations beyond our control, yes, but the ones in or under our control, why not do them well? No one is owing you any resources that you should wait for.

My staff used to complain whenever the warehouse did not supply materials to my branch, hence, we end up buying from the local market which was more expensive. As a result, my staff blame the warehouse even for poor sales.

I called the sectional heads and explained to them that we sometimes produce late that's why we have low sales. Then they understood that we were all responsible for low sales, and not the warehouse.

If you wait on government or that your uncle, you might never start such business just as you are yet to start now. The best you can do is to not wait for anyone.

REASON 7

YOU CRITICIZES SUCCESSFUL BUSINESS OWNERS!

I don't know about other countries, but in Nigeria, it is easily assumed that most successful business owners use fetish means such as charms – what we call; "Juju" hence, it is one of the mediums for criticism.

Other mediums of criticism include the complaint of bribery, political influence on policy making to favor desired businesspeople, etc. These complaints are possibly part of the reasons you feel business will not favor you.

Many intending business owners finds it easy to speak against successful business owners than why they should even start their own business. They think that the existence of successful business owners is the reason they are not successful in life.

A good example is the Africa's richest man – Aliko Dangote. Most people say he is a monopolist, he bribes the government to favor his business, his trucks are spoiling our roads in the country, etc. Funny enough, people who make such complaints believes it's because of bad road they can't succeed in business, and so, they don't even try.

Are you like this?

Sincerely check yourself. No one will tell you the truth about you better than you. If you are like this, quickly have a mindset shift.

You won't really start that business if you are the type that complain about successful business owner's faults.

REASON 8

WAITING FOR THE PERFECT TIME, MONEY, AND PLACE TO START

Let me surprise you here:

There are people who already have the capital they need but are waiting for the right time and place to start a business.

There are also those who have the perfect time to start a business, but they don't have the money. And,

There are those who have the right place (site) to establish a business but don't have the money and time as well.

Which are you?

Now, here is the shocking fact about business; there is no perfect time, money, or place to start a business. Don't get me wrong, site is important, but still, there is no perfect site. These are just excuses on why you are yet to start a business.

You don't have to wait until you have a complete amount to start a business. You also don't have to wait for any perfect time or place. The fact that you are a living being and possesses the right skill/knowledge is enough.

Waiting to have a bulk money is a time-wasting attitude that leads to procrastination. And **procrastination** is another obvious reason why you are yet to start a business today.

Sometimes, capital source strategy is just what you need. If so, you can get my strategies; **"How To Raise Money To Start A Business"**

REASON 9

YOU DON'T HAVE A BUSINESS ROLE MODEL

Having a business role model is as important as the business itself.

From the first day I encountered Mrs. Noela Ugwu speaking, I saw myself in her as a corporate trainer. I have been watching several speakers and trainers on YouTube, Facebook, and LinkedIn, but the first day I experienced her, I said to myself, this is it.

I followed her on LinkedIn because she was far from me. I kept learning from her few LinkedIn contents. She's one of the role models I have in the corporate training aspect. Other people I learn from are Emeka Nobis, Nnamdi Ibe, Akin Alabi, etc. *(through their materials).*

What about you?

Oh! how can you even have a role model when you usually criticize successful businesspeople?

I believe you now understand the implication, right?

It's simple. If you don't have someone with the results you admire and dreaming to achieve, how can you be guided? These personalities are not to make you successful, but they serve as guides either directly or indirectly.

Some of them may not know you have them as role models, but their success inspires you. Just like Mrs. Noela, she doesn't know I have her in my list, yet her works keeps inspiring me.

So, the question is; **Who is your business role model?**

REASON 10

YOU DON'T HAVE THE RIGHT PEOPLE AROUND YOU

You are probably thinking you don't need anyone around you to successfully start and succeed in business, right? motivational speakers told you that.

Well, they only said that so you can learn to first, believe in yourself and remove low self-esteem. Remember we said that fear of loss can also result from low self-esteem. Feeling you can't do it.

So, this is what motivational speakers meant, that "you can do it." Whatever you put your mind in, you can achieve it. But hey, you need people to achieve this.

You still need someone who can motivate you to start. Someone like a lover, siblings, niblings, parents, aunt, spouse, etc. Even prospective customers can motivate you to start a business so they can patronize you, because they also need the product to survive. You need the encouragement. It's a booster.

But what about when you don't have anyone? It become extremely difficult to start. It's a reality you cannot skip. Hence, to overcome this and start a business, you need to start developing meaningful connections wherever possible.

Everything about life itself works with connection. Bear that in mind as you journey in life.

SUMMARY

Starting a business can be difficult, especially when;

- You are yet to decide,
- You don't have a good reason,
- You have a job,
- You are afraid of loss,
- You don't have the required skill/knowledge,
- You are waiting for government to give you grant,
- You criticize successful business owners,
- You are waiting for the perfect money, time, and place,
- You don't have a business role model, and,
- You don't have the right people around you.

However, you can still start now if you make the decision and follow other processes that can make you successful. It's fully up to you to decide today.

Want to book a session with me?

Email: eliasfrancis735@gmail.com

WhatsApp: https://wa.me/2347058810203

Now, let's start your business!

www.ingramcontent.com/pod-product-compliance
Lightning Source LLC
Chambersburg PA
CBHW070959220526
45471CB00007B/3093